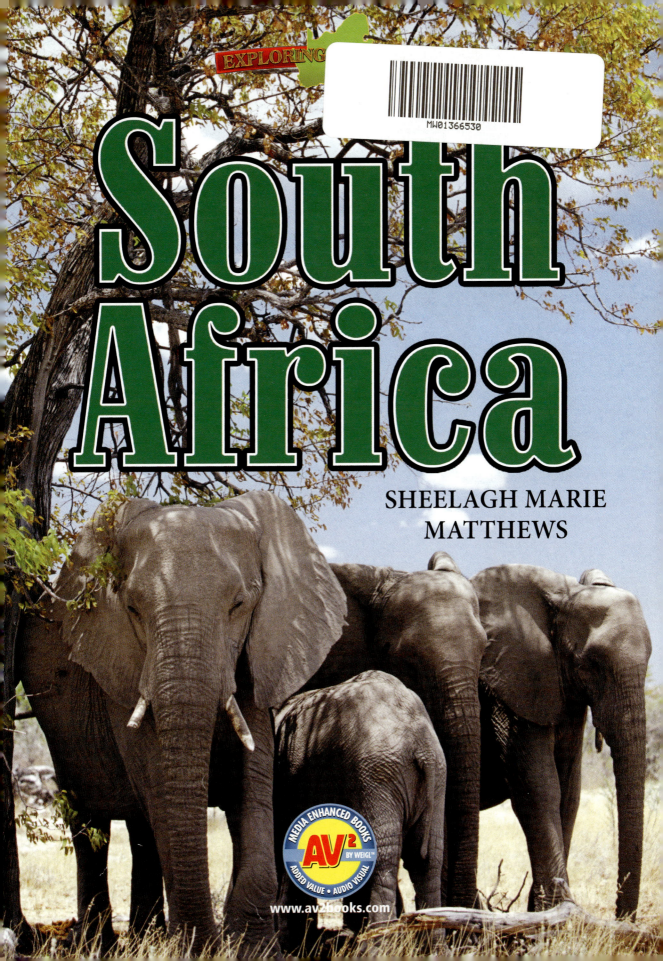

EXPLORING

South Africa

SHEELAGH MARIE MATTHEWS

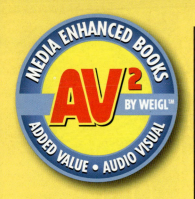

AV² provides enriched content that supplements and complements this book. Weigl's AV² books strive to create inspired learning and engage young minds in a total learning experience.

Your AV² Media Enhanced books come alive with...

 Audio
Listen to sections of the book read aloud.

J9168
MAT
C.1

 Key Words
Study vocabulary, and complete a matching word activity.

Go to www.av2books.com, and enter this book's unique code.

 Video
Watch informative video clips.

 Quizzes
Test your knowledge.

BOOK CODE

X747745

 Embedded Weblinks
Gain additional information for research.

 Slide Show
View images and captions, and prepare a presentation.

AV² by Weigl brings you media enhanced books that support active learning.

 **Try This!**
Complete activities and hands-on experiments.

... and much, much more!

Published by AV² by Weigl
350 5th Avenue, 59th Floor
New York, NY 10118
Websites: www.av2books.com   www.weigl.com

Copyright © 2015 AV² by Weigl
All rights reserved. No part of this publication may be reproduced, stored in a retrieval system, or transmitted in any form or by any means, electronic, mechanical, photocopying, recording, or otherwise, without the prior written permission of the publisher.

Library of Congress Cataloging-in-Publication Data

Matthews, Sheelagh.
  South Africa / Sheelagh Matthews.
     pages cm. — (Exploring countries)
Includes index.
  ISBN 978-1-4896-1030-0 (hardcover : alk. paper) — ISBN 978-1-4896-1031-7 (softcover : alk. paper) —
  ISBN 978-1-4896-1032-4 (single user ebk.) — ISBN 978-1-4896-1033-1 (multi user ebk.)
  1. South Africa—Juvenile literature. I. Title.
  DT1719.M38 2014
  968—dc23
                                  2014005946

Printed in the United States of America in North Mankato, Minnesota
1 2 3 4 5 6 7 8 9 0 18 17 16 15 14

042014
WEP150314

Project Coordinator Heather Kissock
Art Director Terry Paulhus

Photo Credits
Every reasonable effort has been made to trace ownership and to obtain permission to reprint copyright material. The publishers would be pleased to have any errors or omissions brought to their attention so that they may be corrected in subsequent printings.

Weigl acknowledges Getty Images as its primary image supplier for this title.

Contents

AV² Book Code 2	Early Settlers 18
South Africa Overview 4	Population 20
Exploring South Africa 6	Politics and Government 21
Land and Climate 8	Cultural Groups 22
Plants and Animals 10	Arts and Entertainment 24
Natural Resources 11	Sports 26
Tourism 12	Mapping South Africa 28
Industry 14	Quiz Time 30
Goods and Services 15	Key Words 31
Indigenous Peoples 16	Index 31
The Age of Exploration 17	Log on to www.av2books.com 32

South Africa Overview

Located on the southern tip of Africa, the Republic of South Africa is a country known for its natural beauty, its diamond mines, and President Nelson Mandela. In 1994, he helped end the 46-year period of **apartheid**. Today, South Africa's laws give all of its people equal rights. From its people to its land and animal life, South Africa is a nation of great diversity. Its rich natural resources give the country one of the largest **economies** in Africa.

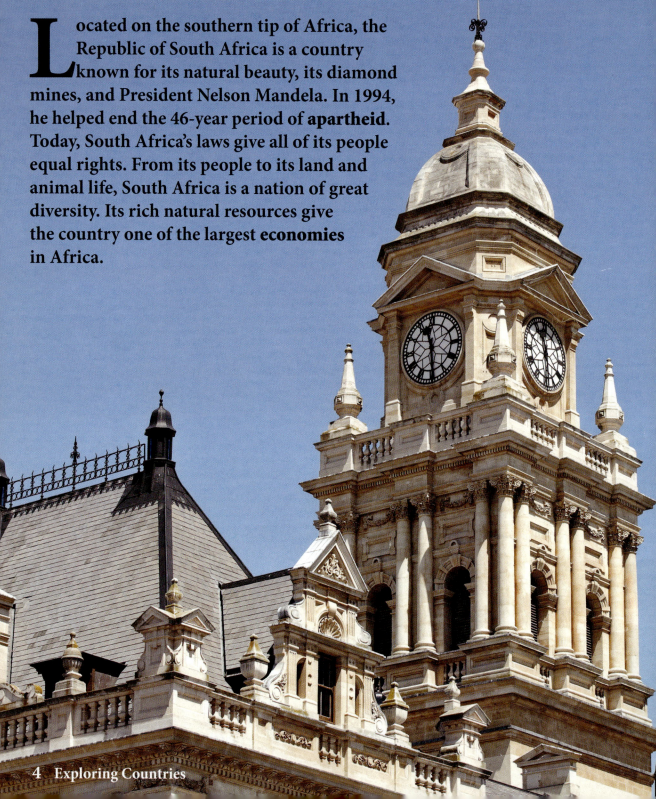

Tugela Falls, in eastern South Africa, is 3,110 feet (950 meters) tall, making it the highest waterfall in Africa.

April 27 is Freedom Day, a national holiday to celebrate the ending of apartheid.

Many types of animals live in South Africa, including leopards.

Diamonds have been mined in South Africa since the 1800s.

The country's millions of sports fans blow long horns called vuvuzelas to cheer on their team.

South Africa 5

Exploring South Africa

South Africa is bordered by the Atlantic Ocean in the west and the Indian Ocean in the east. The countries of Namibia, Botswana, Zimbabwe, Mozambique, and Swaziland lie to the north and northeast. South Africa completely surrounds the country of Lesotho. South Africa also controls Prince Edward Island and Marion Island in the southern Indian Ocean. With a total area of 470,693 square miles (1,219,090 square kilometers), South Africa is about one-eighth the size of the United States. Its coastline stretches for more than 1,700 miles (2,800 kilometers).

Orange River

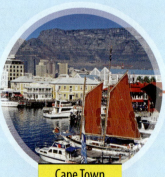
Cape Town

Cape Town

Cape Town is the country's oldest city founded by European settlers. As the legislative capital of South Africa, Cape Town is where the nation's parliament meets. More than 3.5 million people live in the city.

Map Legend

- South Africa
- Orange River
- Capital City
- Land
- Drakensberg
- Water
- Kruger National Park

SCALE 250 Miles / 250 Kilometers

6 Exploring Countries

Orange River

The Orange River is South Africa's longest river and one of the longest rivers in Africa. Starting in the Drakensberg mountain range, it flows west to the Atlantic Ocean. The river forms part of the boundary between Namibia and South Africa.

Drakensberg

The Drakensberg is South Africa's highest mountain range, with peaks more than 11,400 feet (3,475 m) tall. The mountains extend from north to south near the Indian Ocean coast. Drawings made by ancient peoples thousands of years ago can be seen on some of the region's rocks and cave walls.

Kruger National Park

The first national park created in South Africa, Kruger covers more than 7,500 square miles (19,000 sq. km). The land is flat, with some low hills, and varies from open plains to regions covered by bushes and trees. People from around the world visit Kruger to see and photograph the many **species** of animals that live in this protected area.

LAND AND CLIMATE

South Africa features sweeping valleys, huge plains, rugged mountains, inland deserts, and coastal beaches. A specific area's climate depends on its elevation and location. The entire country, however, receives a great deal of sunshine.

A high **plateau** stretches across the interior of South Africa. Bushveld covers one-third of this flat land. *Veld* is the **Afrikaans** word for a natural area of land. Bushveld describes natural areas of grasses and bushes. During the winter months of May to July, the plateau has cool, dry, sunny days. Temperatures can drop below freezing at night.

The Blyde River canyon in eastern South Africa is one of the largest canyons in the world.

The Great Karoo is a plateau of grasslands in southern South Africa that receives very little rain. This region's name means "land of great thirst." Light summer rains follow dry winter months there.

The Twelve Apostles mountain range lies along the Atlantic Coast south of Cape Town.

8 Exploring Countries

The Kalahari Desert extends across three countries. It covers part of northwestern South Africa, most of eastern Namibia, and a large portion of Botswana. The Kalahari receives small amounts of rainfall, which allows the region to support some plant and animal life. It has no surface water, however, since most rain sinks into the Kalahari's deep, reddish-colored sand.

The Great Escarpment is a ridge that separates South Africa's low coastal areas from the interior plateau. The Drakensberg makes up part of this ridge. Over millions of years, **erosion** created huge cliffs in this region.

Forests are the smallest **ecosystems** in South Africa. They often cover small areas where rainfall is high and temperatures remain above freezing. South Africa's forests are home to colorful birds and lush plant life.

Land and Climate by the Numbers

360,000 Square Miles
Size of the Kalahari Desert. (930,000 sq. km)

700 Miles
Length of the Drakensberg. (1,125 km)

More Than 65%
Portion of the country made up of the interior plateau.

PLANTS AND ANIMALS

South Africa has so many species of plants and animals that the group Conservation International declared the country to be one of 17 **megadiverse** places in the world. More than 8,500 plant species grow in just one part of the Cape region near the country's southern tip. To safeguard these species, eight protected areas have been set up in the region. These areas were named a World Heritage Site by **UNESCO**.

Baobab trees are found in many parts of South Africa. These trees are known for their huge trunks. The trunk can store large amounts of water, which helps the baobab survive in dry climates.

The waters off South Africa's coast are home to many types of sea life. Southern right whales **migrate** to South Africa from Antarctica each June. Penguins live along the Atlantic coastline.

South Africa's land animals include rhinoceroses, elephants, lions, leopards, and buffaloes. These are the so-called Big Five that people taking **safaris** tend to be most interested in seeing. The country's varied animal life also includes giraffes, zebras, cheetahs, antelopes, hippopotamuses, hyenas, meerkats, and monkeys.

Giraffes live in many parts of South Africa. The tallest land animals in the world, they can grow to more than 18 feet (5.5 m) high.

Plants and Animals BY THE NUMBERS

About 75 feet
Width of the largest baobab tree trunks. (23 m)

10,000 Number of plant and animal species found in South Africa's coastal waters.

800 Number of bird species seen in South Africa

NATURAL RESOURCES

Fresh water is one of Earth's most valuable natural resources. However, water is not in great supply in South Africa's dry climate. Two main **river systems**, the Orange River and the Limpopo River, supply the nation with water for drinking, agriculture, and other needs. Farming accounts for about half the water used in South Africa.

Only about 10 percent of South Africa's land is suitable for farming. Maize, or corn, is the main crop. South Africa is the world's 10th largest producer of sunflower seeds and the 13th largest sugar producer.

The nation has rich supplies of many valuable minerals, including gold, diamonds, and platinum. South Africa is the fifth-largest diamond-producing country in the world. The Witwatersrand mountain ridge, in the northeastern part of the country, is known for its gold-bearing rock.

While South Africa's natural forests are small, the country has more land used for plantation forests than any other African nation. Plantation forests are areas planted with a single type of tree. The trees are then harvested for their lumber.

Natural Resources by the Numbers

5th South Africa's rank among the world's largest producers of gold.

3.7 Million Acres
Amount of land in South Africa used for plantation forests. (1.49 million hectares)

1,300 miles Length of the Orange River. (2,100 km)

The Vanderkloof Dam on the Orange River is used to produce electricity and to collect water that is then used for farming.

TOURISM

South Africa welcomes millions of tourists each year. They come to enjoy the country's music, museums, historic sites, and other cultural attractions. Many people are drawn to South Africa to join a safari and see the region's natural beauty. People who enjoy water sports come to South Africa for snorkeling or surfing.

The end of apartheid in 1994 led to an increase in visitors from other countries. Many people are interested in understanding how South Africans changed their political system. The Apartheid Museum in Johannesburg takes visitors on a journey through this period in South Africa's history.

While rhinos can sometimes still be hunted in South Africa, most tourists come to shoot photos of them.

The prison where Nelson Mandela was jailed for 18 years during apartheid is now the Robben Island Museum. It stands as a reminder of the price many South Africans had to pay to gain equal rights. Robben Island is a UNESCO World Heritage Site.

Tourists taking the train along a part of the southeastern coast known as the Garden Route can see wide beaches, shady forests, and busy seaside towns.

Activities such as hiking, camping, and mountain climbing appeal to many visitors. The top of Table Mountain, outside Cape Town, is a favorite destination for climbers. Other tourists take a cable car to enjoy the views from this flat-topped mountain. Almost 1 million people visit Kruger National Park each year. More than 20 other national parks in the country also attract nature lovers and people interested in South Africa's Big Five and other types of animal life.

The cities of South Africa have a great deal to offer, too. Johannesburg became a more popular place to visit after South Africa hosted the 2010 men's World Cup soccer tournament. Television viewers in more than 200 countries watched the championship game, played in Johannesburg's FNB Stadium, which is often called Soccer City. Visitors to Johannesburg may take a guided tour of Soweto, a suburb of the city. Soweto is known for its many places where people can listen and dance to music. The city of Durban, on the east coast, is popular for its beaches and water sports.

Port Elizabeth, on the southeast coast, is nicknamed the Windy City. It attracts sailors and windsurfers.

Tourism by the Numbers

2013 Year U.S. president Barack Obama wrote in the guest book of the Robben Island Museum, "The world is grateful for the heroes of Robben Island."

9.2 Million Number of foreign tourists who visited South Africa in 2012.

MORE THAN 90,000 Number of fans that Soccer City can hold.

INDUSTRY

South Africa is a world leader in mining. While manufacturing employs more people, the mining industry continues to be an important part of the South African economy. Agriculture, forestry, and fishing are also major industries that create jobs.

Diamond mining brings many workers to the area around Kimberley. This city, located in the center of the country, was founded after diamonds were discovered in the region in the 1860s. The De Beers family of farmers owned the land where South Africa's first diamond mine stood. Today, De Beers is one of the world's largest companies mining and selling diamonds.

The hardest known substance on Earth, diamonds have many uses. Industrial diamonds are used for cutting, grinding, drilling, and polishing. Diamonds are also the world's most popular gemstone for jewelry.

Metals mined in South Africa include iron and chromium, as well as platinum and gold. The country has many of the world's largest known deposits of gold. In 2012, this metal was South Africa's biggest mineral **export**.

Industry by the Numbers

3 Tons Weight of diamonds produced by "The Big Hole" diamond mine before it closed in 1914. (2.7 tonnes)

1 Million Number of jobs in South Africa related to mining.

2.2 Miles Depth of the Mponeng gold mine near Johannesburg, the deepest mine in the world. (3.5 km)

Men using only picks and shovels dug the Big Hole mine near Kimberley. It is one of the largest human-made holes on Earth.

GOODS AND SERVICES

Goods made in South Africa include electronics products, chemicals, **textiles**, and processed foods. The automobile industry is important to the country's economy. Manufacturers such as Ford, Volkswagen, General Motors, Mercedes Benz, and Toyota all produce cars or auto parts in South Africa.

Farmers raise many kinds of vegetables and fruits, including grapes used for wine. South Africa is the world's eighth-largest wine producing country. Most South African wine is made in the region around Cape Town.

More South African workers are employed in the service industry than any other. People in this industry provide a service rather than produce goods. Service workers include people employed in banks, schools, hospitals, stores, restaurants, and hotels. As tourism has grown, more South Africans are finding jobs serving the country's visitors.

South Africa's **telecommunications** industry is the most modern in Africa. Cellular telephone service is widely available. Access to the internet is common in **urban** areas but more difficult to obtain in the countryside.

> Most automobile factories are in the Eastern Cape Province, in the southeastern part of the country.

Goods and Services BY THE NUMBERS

65% Portion of South African workers employed in the service industry.

135 Number of cell phones per 100 people in South Africa.

41% Portion of the population that has access to the internet.

INDIGENOUS PEOPLES

Indigenous Peoples by the Numbers

2.5 Million Years Old
Estimated age of a skull found by archaeologists in the Cradle of Humankind.

25 to 60
Number of people in a traditional band of San people.

40% Portion of South Africans who speak either IsiZulu or IsiXhosa, the languages of the Zulu and Xhosa peoples.

Archaeologists have found evidence that **ancestors** of present-day humans may have lived in what is now South Africa as early as 3 million years ago. A valley near Johannesburg is known as the Cradle of Humankind. Bones discovered there by scientists are millions of years old.

The San people, who were called Bushmen by European settlers, have lived in today's South Africa for about 20,000 years. They roamed the countryside, hunting animals and gathering plants for food. The San had no permanent homes, but they built shelters as needed.

The Khoekhoe people came to the region from present-day Botswana in about 100 AD. The name Khoekhoe, also spelled Khoikhoi, means "men of men." These people were farmers, raising sheep and cattle. Together, the San and Khoekhoe peoples are called the Khoisan.

Bantu-speaking people moved south into eastern regions of what is now South Africa about 1,800 years ago. These people kept herds of cattle. They were also skilled at making pottery, as well as iron tools.

The Zulu people of South Africa are **descendants** of the Nguni, a Bantu-speaking group. They lived in small groups where they farmed and kept cattle. South Africa's Xhosa people also are descended from the Nguni.

Many Xhosa people build huts of mud and thatch, a mixture of dried grasses and leaves.

THE AGE OF EXPLORATION

During the 1400s, Portuguese explorers were searching for a trade route by sea from Europe to East Asia. In 1488, they sailed around a point of land near Africa's southern tip, which they named the Cape of Good Hope. They did not settle in the region, however. By the 1500s, several other European nations were also seeking a sea route between Europe and Asia.

English explorer Francis Drake reached the Cape of Good Hope on June 15, 1580. He was sailing around the world on behalf of Queen Elizabeth I. By the 1590s, both Dutch and English ships were stopping at Table Bay, just north of the Cape of Good Hope. The sailors needed to restock their vessels with food and water. They traded goods for food with the Khoekhoe people living in the area.

Soon after, the Dutch East India Company was created. The Dutch government allowed this company to control the country's trade with Asia. The voyage between the Netherlands and East Asia took about six months, so the company decided it needed a regular place to restock its ships. Dutch merchant Jan van Riebeeck, who worked for the company, founded Cape Town in 1652. Van Riebeeck used slaves from Asia to help build a fort.

The Age of Exploration BY THE NUMBERS

1577–1580 Years when Francis Drake sailed around the world.

1602 Year the Dutch East India Company was founded.

1713 Year that smallpox, a disease brought to the Cape region by Dutch sailors, began to kill many Khoekhoe people.

The Dutch East India Company raised livestock to supply meat to the many ships stopping at Cape Town.

EARLY SETTLERS

The Voortrekker Monument and Nature Reserve in Pretoria honors the Boers' Great Trek.

Cape Town and the area around it, called the Dutch Cape **Colony**, attracted settlers from the Netherlands. Early settlers were known as Boers, a Dutch word for "farmers." When the Boers wanted fields to graze cattle, they forced the native peoples off the land. The Boers brought slaves from Asia to help them farm.

After a war in Europe between Great Britain and the Netherlands, the Cape Colony came under British control in 1806. Great Britain ended slavery in the colony. Many Boers did not want to live under British rule. In the late 1830s, after secretly selling their land, they set off on what became known as the Great Trek.

Boer trekkers, as they were called, moved from coastal areas into the interior. They used force to take land and cattle from the native peoples living in the regions where they settled. The Boers set up the Orange Free State and the South African Republic, or the Transvaal. They declared these two areas independent of Great Britain.

About 12,000 to 14,000 Boers traveled in the Great Trek.

During the 1800s, British settlers moved to the Cape Colony and other areas in southern Africa. Great Britain tried to gain control of all of today's South Africa. In 1879, British troops invaded Zulu lands. About 40,000 Zulu warriors defending their kingdom stopped the British at first. By late 1879, however, the war ended in victory for the British.

Great Britain then tried to gain control of the Orange Free State and the Transvaal. British troops fought two wars against Boer settlers. The conflict known as the First Boer War took place from 1880 to 1881. The Second Boer War was fought from 1899 to 1902.

Great Britain won the Second Boer War. The British now had control over four areas. They were the Cape Colony, the Transvaal, the Orange Free State, and Natal, the region that had been the Zulu kingdom.

In 1910, these four areas became the Union of South Africa. Great Britain gave the Union self-government. In 1948, the National Party came to power in South Africa. This party created the apartheid system that divided the country for the next 46 years.

Early Settlers BY THE NUMBERS

500,000
Total number of British soldiers who fought in South Africa during the Second Boer War.

88,000
Number of Boer fighters during the Second Boer War.

2 Number of official languages, English and Afrikaans, in the Union of South Africa during its early years.

The Battle of Isandlwana on January 11, 1879, was a major British defeat early in the Zulu War.

South Africa 19

POPULATION

In 2014, South Africa's population was about 48.4 million. Almost four-fifths of the country's people are black. About 10 percent are white, and nearly 3 percent are of Indian or other Asian ancestry.

Many people live in urban areas. Johannesburg, the country's largest city, has a population of more than 3.8 million. About 3 million people live in Durban.

During apartheid, most black South Africans did not have access to high-quality education, well-paying jobs, or good medical care. Black South Africans tended to be very poor. Both poverty and health problems remain major issues for the country today.

Life expectancy is short in South Africa. On average, people live to only about 50 years old. This figure is lower than the average length of life in almost every other country in the world. The lung disease tuberculosis is common in South Africa. Many people have illnesses resulting from unclean drinking water. Nearly 18 percent of adults in the country suffer from **HIV/AIDS**.

Population by the Numbers

9% Portion of South Africa's people who have mixed-race ancestry.

28% Percentage of South Africans who are less than 15 years old.

6 Million Number of people in South Africa with HIV/AIDS, more than in any other country of the world.

One-third of South Africans are poor, and many people cannot afford good housing.

POLITICS AND GOVERNMENT

During the period of apartheid, the African National Congress (ANC), an organization formed in 1912, led the struggle to improve the rights and living conditions of black South Africans. When apartheid ended, South Africa held a national election in which people of all races were allowed to vote. ANC leader Nelson Mandela became the country's first black president.

South Africa's current **constitution** took effect in 1997. The country is divided into nine provinces. The national and provincial governments share political power.

The national parliament is made up of two houses. Voters elect the 400 members of one house, the National Assembly. The legislatures of the nine provinces elect the 90 members of the other house, the National Council of Provinces. The National Assembly elects the country's president from among its members.

The country's highest courts are the Constitutional Court and the Supreme Court of Appeal. The Constitutional Court reviews laws passed by parliament to make sure they agree with the constitution. The Supreme Court reviews decisions by lower courts.

As president, Nelson Mandela tried to reunite the country after apartheid.

Politics and Government BY THE NUMBERS

1994–1999
Years that Nelson Mandela was president.

18 Years Old
Age at which people are allowed to vote in South Africa.

3 Number of capital cities in South Africa. They are Cape Town, Pretoria, where the president works, and Bloemfontein, where the Supreme Court of Appeal meets.

South Africa 21

CULTURAL GROUPS

Road signs are sometimes in both English and Afrikaans.

South Africa is sometimes called the Rainbow Nation because of its cultural diversity. The country now has 11 official languages. These include the languages of nine groups of native peoples, as well as English and Afrikaans. Most South Africans speak more than one language.

IsiZulu is the first language of more people than any other. English is the most common language used in business offices. Afrikaans is widely spoken by descendants of early Dutch settlers, as well as settlers from Germany and France. In the 17th century, French Protestants were treated harshly in their home country. Some of these people, known as Huguenots, left France to settle in the Dutch Cape Colony.

Independent African church groups range in size from several people to millions. They follow the Christian religion.

In the 19th century, after Great Britain ended slavery, people from India and other areas of Asia were brought to South Africa as **indentured servants**. They mainly worked on sugar plantations. Today, most South Africans of Asian descent speak English as their first language.

More than 80 percent of South Africans are Christian, with about 36 percent belonging to Protestant churches. About 7 percent of South Africans are Catholic. Many black Christians also follow the traditions of ancient African religions. They believe that their ancestors continue to affect their daily life, and they perform ceremonies to honor the dead.

Many black South Africans seek advice from traditional healers called sangomas, as well as from doctors. Sangomas believe that people's ancestors play a role in dealing with various illnesses, both physical and mental. Traditional healers often use natural medicines, made from ingredients such as herbs and tree roots, to help with diseases.

Popular foods in South Africa are as diverse as the country's people. *Biltong* is a type of dried salted meat common in the region long before European settlers arrived. *Boerewors* is a kind of sausage introduced by Europeans. Vegetables that are often eaten include pumpkin, which is native to southern Africa, and corn, which is made into a porridge called mealie pap.

Cultural Groups BY THE NUMBERS

14% Percentage of the people who speak Afrikaans.

1688–1707 Years when most of the Huguenots who moved to South Africa arrived.

2% Portion of South Africans who are Muslims, or followers of the religion Islam.

The Xhosa people often cook traditional meals in large iron pots. One popular Xhosa dish is a mixture of corn, beans, and spices.

South Africa 23

Arts and Entertainment

Nhlanhla Nciza and Theo Kgosinkwe make up the group Mafikizolo.

During apartheid, both black and white artists were put in prison or forced to leave the country if the government objected to their work. Native African art was considered inferior to traditional European art. Some people had to secretly display their works, play their music, or publish their literature. Now, artists of all types are free to create, show, and perform new works.

Many types of music are popular in South Africa, including classical, jazz, rock, hip-hop, and pop. Kwaito is a style of dance music that originated in Soweto in the 1990s and includes traditional African rhythms. A newer kind of Soweto music called Shangaan electro speeds up the rhythm to get dancers moving faster.

The singing group called Mafikizolo has fans both in South Africa and around the world. Their songs and music videos have been nominated for international music awards. The group's recordings include new versions of songs performed by Miriam Makeba.

Singers and dancers perform traditional music in Soweto and other areas.

Exploring Countries

Beginning in the 1960s, Makeba played a major role in making South African musical styles known worldwide. She was called Mama Africa and the Empress of African Song. Makeba opposed apartheid, and for many years, she was not allowed to return to South Africa. She recorded and performed mostly in the United States and Europe, including with American singers Harry Belafonte and Paul Simon.

Writer Athol Fugard is well known for his plays criticizing apartheid. His works look at the effects of this policy on both black and white South Africans. Many of his plays have been performed in the United States and Europe, as well as in South Africa. Fugard has also acted in films and plays.

Novelist J. M. Coetzee writes about the effects of apartheid and European colonization of South Africa. He has won many awards for his books, including a Nobel Prize. Coetzee has also taught at universities in South Africa, the United States, and Australia.

Arts and Entertainment BY THE NUMBERS

1995 Year that the annual South African Music Awards, known as the SAMAs, began.

More Than 50 Years Length of Miriam Makeba's singing career.

2003 Year that J. M. Coetzee won the Nobel Prize in Literature.

Athol Fugard's play *Blood Knot* tells the story of two brothers with different fathers. It explores racism.

Sports

South Africans enjoy playing and watching sports. Young and old, men and women alike come out to cheer their favorite teams. Soccer, better known as football in South Africa, is the country's most popular sport. Fans at a match often wear clothing and face paint in their team's colors.

Rugby, introduced by the British, is also very popular. In 1995, South Africa competed for the first time in the rugby World Cup, and the country also hosted the tournament. On June 24, about 65,000 fans in Johannesburg cheered South Africa's national team, the Springboks, as it defeated New Zealand in the final match to win the championship. President Nelson Mandela publicly supported the Springboks, which had only white players. His action was a step toward unifying the country soon after the end of apartheid.

Led by captain François Pienaar, South Africa's rugby team celebrated its 1995 World Cup victory.

Cricket was also introduced by British settlers. One of South Africa's most successful players in recent years was Makhaya Ntini, who retired in 2011. He was the first black cricketer to play for the South African national team, nicknamed the Proteas.

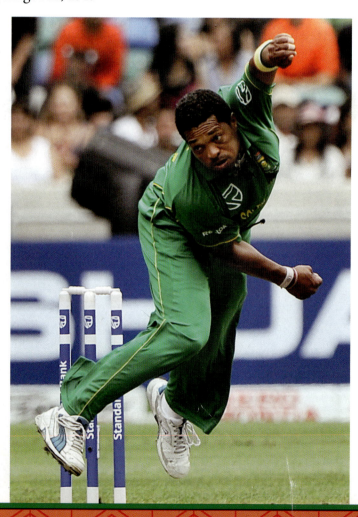

Makhaya Ntini bowled, or pitched, for South Africa's national cricket team.

The Comrades Marathon is held each year between the cities of Durban and Pietermaritzburg. First held in 1921, the race covers a distance of about 56 miles (89 km). Runners from around the world turn out to compete in the event. They must complete the course within 12 hours, but the best winning times have been under 5.5 hours.

Cape Town is the starting point for the South Atlantic Yacht Race, between South Africa and South America. It is the longest continent-to-continent yacht race held in the southern hemisphere. Boaters from around the world compete in the event, which was first held in 1971. It is also known as the Cape to Rio Race, because it often ends in the city of Rio de Janeiro, Brazil.

In 2013, South Africa's Claude Moshiywa had the fastest time in the Comrades Marathon, finishing the race in 5 hours, 32 minutes, and 9 seconds.

Sports by the Numbers

2007 Year South Africa won the rugby World Cup for the second time.

3,900 TO 5,200 MILES Length of the South Atlantic Yacht Race. (6,280 to 8,370 km)

18,000 Number of runners taking part in the Comrades Marathon.

Mapping South Africa

We use many tools to interpret maps and to understand the locations of features such as cities, provinces, lakes, and rivers. The map below has many tools to help interpret information on the map of South Africa.

Mapping Tools

- The compass rose shows north, south, east, and west. The points in between represent northeast, northwest, southeast, and southwest.
- The map scale shows that the distances on a map represent much longer distances in real life. If you measure the distance between objects on a map, you can use the map scale to calculate the actual distance in miles or kilometers between those two points.
- The lines of latitude and longitude are long lines that appear on maps. The lines of latitude run east to west and measure how far north or south of the equator a place is located. The lines of longitude run north to south and measure how far east or west of the Prime Meridian a place is located. A location on a map can be found by using the two numbers where latitude and longitude meet. This number is called a coordinate and is written using degrees and direction. For example, the city of Cape Town would be found at 34°S and 18°E on a map.

Map It!

Using the map and the appropriate tools, complete the activities below.

Locating with latitude and longitude
1. What city is located at 26°S and 28°E?
2. What body of water is located at 34°S and 18°E?
3. Which South African river is at about latitude 28°S?

Distances between points
4. Using the map scale and a ruler, calculate the approximate distance between the cities of Cape Town and Bloemfontein.
5. Using the map scale and a ruler, calculate the approximate length of the Vaal River.
6. Using the map scale and a ruler, find the approximate distance from Pretoria to Durban.

ANSWERS 1. Johannesburg 2. Cape of Good Hope 3. Orange River 4. 570 miles (920 km) 5. 750 miles (1,200 km) 6. 400 miles (645 km)

Quiz Time

Test your knowledge of South Africa by answering these questions.

1 What animals make up South Africa's Big Five?

2 How big is South Africa compared to the United States?

3 In what year did apartheid end?

4 What is the name of South Africa's first black president?

5 What is the name for early settlers from the Netherlands?

6 What is South Africa's main crop?

7 What is the most popular sport in South Africa?

8 Soweto is a suburb of which South African city?

9 How much of South Africa's land can be farmed?

10 What is the name of the singer who was known as Mama Africa?

ANSWERS
1. Rhinoceroses, elephants, lions, leopards, and buffaloes
2. One-eighth the size of the United States
3. 1994
4. Nelson Mandela
5. Boers
6. Corn, also known as maize
7. Soccer, also known as football
8. Johannesburg
9. About 10 percent
10. Miriam Makeba

Key Words

Afrikaans: a form of the Dutch language spoken in South Africa
ancestors: people related to present-day people and who lived long ago
apartheid: a legal policy separating whites and nonwhites that gave nonwhites fewer rights and limited their opportunities for jobs, housing, and education
archaeologists: scientists who study past human life and cultures
colony: an area or country that is under the control of another country
constitution: a country's basic laws, which state the rights of the people and the powers of the government
descendants: people who share common ancestors
economies: the wealth and resources of countries or areas
ecosystems: local environments and the plants and animals that live in them
erosion: the wearing away of rock and soil by wind and water
export: something a country sells to another country
HIV/AIDS: a disease caused by a virus that attacks the body's immune system
indentured servants: people who sign a contract to work for an individual for a specific time period, often in exchange for housing and food.
megadiverse: having a very large number of native plant and animal species
migrate: move from one place to another at different times of year
plateau: an area of flat land that is higher than the land around it
river systems: large rivers and the tributaries, or smaller rivers, that flow into them
safaris: journeys by a group of people to see or hunt animals
species: groups of individuals with common characteristics
telecommunications: communication over a long distance, such as by telephone, radio, television, or the internet
textiles: woven or knit cloth
UNESCO: the United Nations Educational, Scientific, and Cultural Organization, whose main goals are to promote world peace and eliminate poverty through education, science, and culture
urban: relating to a city or town

Index

African National Congress 21
Afrikaans 8, 9, 22, 23
animals 4, 5, 7, 9, 10, 13, 16, 30
apartheid 4, 5, 12, 19, 20, 21, 24, 25, 26, 30

Big Hole mine 14
Bloemfontein 21, 28, 29
Boers 18, 19, 30
Boer wars 19

Cape of Good Hope 17, 28
Cape Town 6, 8, 13, 15, 17, 21, 27, 28, 29
Coetzee, J. M. 25

diamonds 4, 5, 11, 14
Drake, Francis 17
Drakensberg 6, 7, 9, 28
Durban 13, 20, 27, 28, 29
Dutch Cape Colony 18, 19, 22

economy 4, 14, 15

farming 11, 14, 15, 16, 18, 30
foods 15, 16, 17, 23
forests 9, 11, 12, 14
Fugard, Athol 25

gold 11, 14
Great Britain 18, 19, 23
Great Karoo 8

HIV/AIDS 20

indigenous peoples 7, 16, 17, 18, 22
industries 14, 15

Johannesburg 12, 13, 14, 16, 20, 26, 28, 29, 30

Kalahari Desert 9
Khoekhoe 16, 17
Kimberley 14, 28
Kruger National Park 6, 7, 13, 28, 29

languages 8, 16, 19, 22, 23
Limpopo River 11, 28

Makeba, Miriam 24, 25, 30
Mandela, Nelson 4, 12, 21, 26, 30
mining 4, 5, 11, 14
music 12, 13, 24, 25

Obama, Barack 13
Orange Free State 18, 19
Orange River 6, 7, 11, 28, 29

plants 9, 10, 11, 16
population 13, 20
Port Elizabeth 13, 28
Portugal 17
poverty 20
Pretoria 21, 28, 29

religions 22, 23
Robben Island 12, 13

San 16
Soweto 13, 24, 30
sports 5, 12, 13, 26, 27, 30

telecommunications 15
tourism 12, 13, 15
Transvaal 18, 19

UNESCO 10, 12

van Riebeeck, Jan 16, 17

water 5, 9, 10, 11, 12, 13, 17, 20
Witwatersrand 11

Xhosa 16, 23

Zulu 16, 18, 19

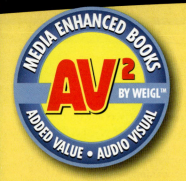

Log on to www.av2books.com

AV² by Weigl brings you media enhanced books that support active learning. Go to www.av2books.com, and enter the special code found on page 2 of this book. You will gain access to enriched and enhanced content that supplements and complements this book. Content includes video, audio, weblinks, quizzes, a slide show, and activities.

AV² Online Navigation

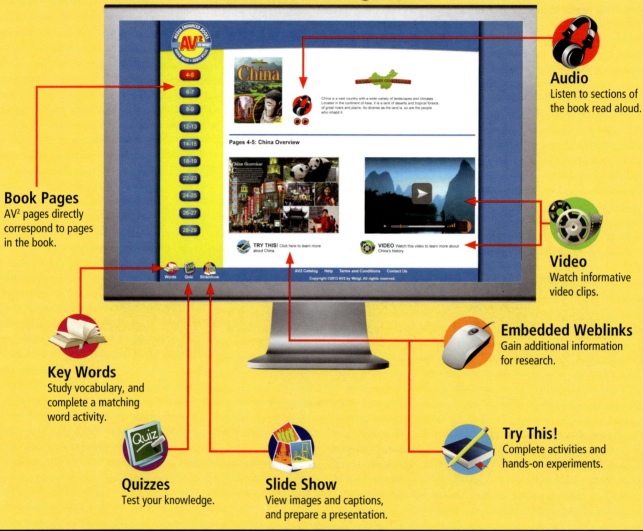

Book Pages
AV² pages directly correspond to pages in the book.

Audio
Listen to sections of the book read aloud.

Video
Watch informative video clips.

Key Words
Study vocabulary, and complete a matching word activity.

Embedded Weblinks
Gain additional information for research.

Quizzes
Test your knowledge.

Slide Show
View images and captions, and prepare a presentation.

Try This!
Complete activities and hands-on experiments.

AV² was built to bridge the gap between print and digital. We encourage you to tell us what you like and what you want to see in the future.

Sign up to be an AV² Ambassador at www.av2books.com/ambassador.

Due to the dynamic nature of the Internet, some of the URLs and activities provided as part of AV² by Weigl may have changed or ceased to exist. AV² by Weigl accepts no responsibility for any such changes. All media enhanced books are regularly monitored to update addresses and sites in a timely manner. Contact AV² by Weigl at 1-866-649-3445 or av2books@weigl.com with any questions, comments, or feedback.